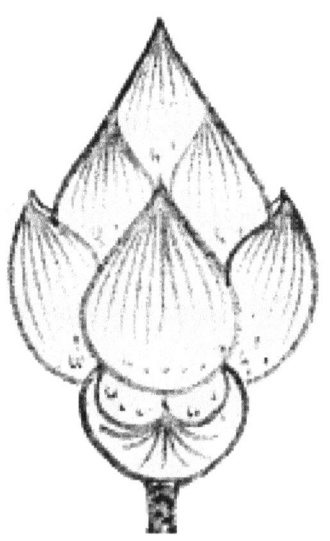

BLUE WHITE VEIL

BLUE WHITE VEIL

Susan B. Gilbert

Black Bamboo Press
Los Angeles, CA

Copyright © 2012 by Susan B. Gilbert
All rights reserved. No part of this book may be replaced or transmitted in any form or by any means, electronic or mechanical, including photocopying, recording, or by any information storage and retrieval system, without permission in writing from the publisher.

Published by Black Bamboo Press
www.blackbamboopress.com

Printed in the United States of America
Cover Design: Sakada

ISBN-13: 978-0-9837284-0-5
ISBN-10: 0983728402

CONTENTS

Acknowledgements	ix
Mortality	1
Melanoma	3
Fortune Teller	5
The Small Dark Spot	6
The Anxiety God	7
ABCDetective	8
No One Seems to Notice	9
My Birthday	11
stratum corneum or the bottom of the outermost layer of skin	12
Tuesday: The Results Show	13
Wheel of Fortune	14
in situ	15
Surgical Oncology	16
The Sharpie	18
Cancer Cells in light of Daniel Ladinsky's renderings of Hafiz poem titled "Someone should start laughing"	19
The Quiet Moments	20
Reactions	21
Tumor World	23
One More Cup of Coffee	24
Winter	25
Post Op	26
Nick of Time	27
Pathology – With a Nod to Coldplay's "Death And All His Friends"	28
Postscript: The Aftermath	29
Peace In Ordinary Time	31
Permissions Page	33

Acknowledgements

First, I want to thank Sakada for her friendship, encouragement and unwavering support, even while pushing me to go deeper. Without her deft hand, this book would not be possible. I also wish to thank the original FYGs: Elgee Tavanlar-Amato and Maryann Russo. Those Saturdays were sacred.

I want to send a special hug to my daughter Anna, who grew up quickly during my diagnosis, and my husband Bruce, who supported this project even though he considers poetry a foreign language.

Last, but by no means least, I want to thank the fortune teller. I hold fast to her words – "Long life."

Mortality

Walking swiftly
    on the ledge
Oblivious to
    the precarious edge

Looking straight,
Side to side
Pelicans sidle along for the ride

        stalking cells,
        silent, unseen

Low rumble
Slight stumble
Scree fall
Dust wall
    the small dark spot appears

Looking down
Bile rises
Air drowns

    in a sea of fear

Below a vortex
Boils the sea
Rocks crop
Vertical drop
    to that space where the line between
    bee stings and honey can not be seen

Now walking more slowly
    on the edge
Painfully aware
    how close the ledge

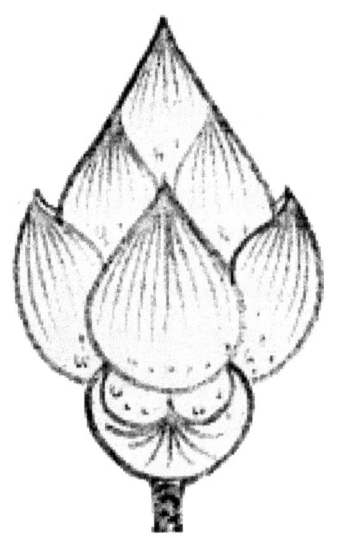

Melanoma

The doctor pointed to the word
in my orange file

        "They call it the blue white veil."

The words rolled around in my head,
conjuring visions:

        icebergs

        Mother Mary

        elderly hair

  that explode

        exposing a deep crevasse,

        stirred, shaken,

        gin with ash

This poetic rendering

        of cancer

lies on top of me

        enters

        I hold tight.

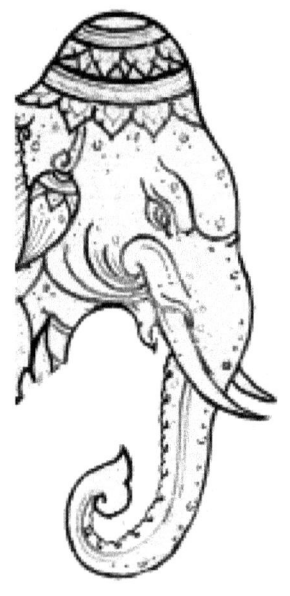

Fortune Teller

                    Fortune Teller
                    Fear queller
                    Cards tatter
                    Skirt frays

Sunday afternoon.
I've just left Café du Monde,
avoiding the fortune tellers in front of St. Louis Cathedral.

                    Doors beckon
                    Whimsical glass
                    Colors reckon
                    Swishing sass

One fortune teller persists, insists.
She takes my hand, I do not resist.
Studying my palms, grinning
"Long life," she says.
"I see no signs of cancer or serious illness."

                    Provocative stance
                    Gypsy dance
                    Bohemian dash
                    Sin and mash

She asks for $50.

Gathering the edges of her skirt
ringed with elephants
she exposes the Empress Tattoo on her calf.

                    Welcome relief
                    Health and peace
                    Aura light
                    Fire flight

I give her $40.

The Small Dark Spot

Crossing my leg,
the small dark spot
has a certain
Je ne sais quoi

Drawing my eye
Barely lit
Visibly screaming
It sits

Suspicious overtones
Ominous groans
"Out damn spot – rub don't blot"
It won't go away

It holds sway

The Anxiety God

Comes at night

Time freezes

He detects
my presence
in the cool, dark sheets

I cannot escape

Holding his sides, he laughs
at the havoc he wreaks

Atoms crowd the room

I spring from my bed
before he suffocates me

ABCDetective

Entering the crime scene

He looks silently at the small dark spot,

A: asymmetrical,
 No two sides alike
B: borders irregular,
 Coloring outside the lines
C: color varied,
 More than one
D: it is almost the size of a pencil eraser
 Splitting hairs
E: evolving.
 Aren't we all?

The clues continue, methodically

I have fair skin and blue eyes
 White knuckles, knees buckle

Looking directly at me
the doctor names the suspect.

No One Seems To Notice

Sitting on the beach,
    I obsess about sun screen

        My family chides me

My legs have never tanned.
    Why worry?

        "I have a spot on my leg.
          I am going to have it checked out."

            There, I've said it.

The world remains intact.
    The words do not.

        They are lost in a sea of sand.
           They bounce off the salt air and disappear.

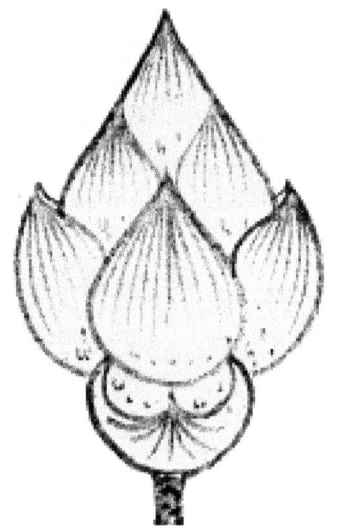

My Birthday

August 1991
Sally brings a gift: A 20 year tarot cycle
Ending with August 2011
The card: Death

>It freaks me out.
>Some gift! Why stop there?
>Sally dismisses my concern.
>She says "Think rebirth, opportunity.
>The card to fear is the Wheel of Fortune"

>I never ask why.

August 2008
The card: Wheel of Fortune

>It registers inwardly.
>Finds a weak spot in the world of numb.
>Think transitions, change –
>Unearthly?

>I wish I had asked why.

stratum corneum
or the bottom of the outermost layer of skin

The dermatologist looks at the spot
   (the leg is one of the most common sites for melanoma in women)

     Play makers, clay bakers, feathers, masks

It now has **all** the characteristics of skin cancer.
   (I silently note that the size is slightly larger.)

     Aging with time, covered in rime

IF it is skin cancer, much will depend upon this biopsy.
   (I clearly remember the fortune teller said no cancer.)

     Creating the moment, wishing it past

He carefully explains:
   (pigment producing melanocytes in the basal layer of the epidermis)

     Scientific rabble, ready for battle

Looking more closely at the small dark spot he mutters - "cell changes."
   (The biopsy hurts - something about trying to get a larger area)

     Border violation, immigrant flirtation

He will know something Tuesday.

"Enjoy your weekend."

"I will."

"Don't worry", he adds.

     Bobby McFerrin sings in my head.
        The Fortune Teller dances to his words.

Tuesday: The Results Show

I call the doctor's office.

>*Dim the lights.*

His receptionist puts me off.

"Biopsies done on Thursday won't be back until this coming Thursday."

I insist.

"The doctor said he would know something on Tuesday."

She puts me on hold.

I listen to the music, feeling foolish.

>Scenes are for drama
>Two headed llama's

Then the doctor's voice comes on the line, "Susan?"

"This can't be good."

>Numbness creeps in monotone
>Creates a veil of granite stone

Wheel of Fortune

Black tea, filigree
Delicate – deceptively

Numb respect
Biopsy detects
Blue tangles of melanin

Disbelief
Odd relief
Too much information

Complex layers
Insurance players
Mortality

Shots of tequila
Anesthesia
Reality

Depth of humor
Comic tumor

Melanoma

in situ

The good news
    It is *in situ*
    sigh, too

        Located within
        Up against the rim
        Maintained, contained

The bad news
    Border not clear

        Pressing the limit
        Announcing its presence
        Waiting for prey, pray

Can it be both?

    (I silently remember the change in size. Damn.)

The cure
    Wide excision

        Surgical precision
        Skin collision
        Blood floes, inflammation woes

"Are you sure?"

"The only patients that have died from this stage of melanoma did not have the surgery."

"But the fortune teller," I want to say…

Surgical Oncology

Entering the office
I scan the room

There's a special desk for surgical oncology

These words register just below the dermis
        an exercise in academic frivolity
        cancer is a strong, singular word
        now robed in pageantry

I step up to the desk
and feel eyes on me

I see women with head scarves, mostly alone
frail elderly men, mostly not
There's a sense of unspoken camaraderie

Yet, I feel remarkably healthy and out of place

    I don't belong here!
    There's been a terrible mistake.

I wait
I am called

The doctor rises,
Extends his hand
"What can I do for you?"

The inside of my head implodes.

    What can you do for me?
    WHAT CAN YOU DO FOR ME?
    Why the hell do you think I am here?

You are an oncologist for God 'sake!

I calmly explain that I have been referred for wide excision of a melanoma

*And I shouldn't really be here because the fortune teller told me
I would live a long life. She said no cancer.
I'll just go home now.*

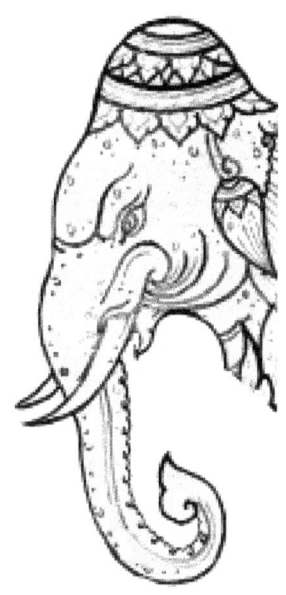

The Sharpie

Tapping the path report
THAT IS RIGHT IN FRONT OF HIM,
He reiterates statistics and margin jargon

I am lucky. My tumor is "thin"

> *Odd juxtaposition for bulging skin*

His words bounce off me and I play with them

> *Thin, win, thankless grin*

lymph nodes –
> *pimp roads, limp rows, who knows?*

In the examining room
He eyes the spot,
> *The spot that used to house the small dark spot, but now looks like a crater drop*
and circles it with a Sharpie.

He asks me to maintain the circle until my surgery because
  Once (*upon a time, a long, long time ago*)
  "They didn't know where to do the wide excision.." he chuckles.

I'm not laughing.
> *I'm staring at the dark black ink now surrounding what used to be the small dark spot and thinking "seriously, a permanent marker?"*

Nerve damage is possible.
It would be permanent –
> *unlike the marker that will wear off even though it is called permanent*

Do I have any questions?
Unbelievably, I say no.

> He doesn't even give me the damn Sharpie.

Cancer Cells in light of Daniel Ladinsky's renderings of Hafiz poem titled "Someone should start laughing"

Perfect sky
Azure blue
Mirror image
Reflecting pool

I have a thousand brilliant lies

Clouds roll in
Stark and white
Subtle reminder
Filtered light

For the question

Overcast's cover
Silver gray
Ominous coming
Judgment day

How are you?

Incision runs
Calf to hip?
Swollen stanzas
Tiny nips

If you think the Sun and the Ocean
Can pass through that tiny opening
Called the mouth

Someone should start wildly Laughing —
Now!

The Quiet Moments

Strong scent
Heightened hum

      Crystal breath

Chipped tile
Breaks the numb

      Widgeons huddle in the mud
      The drake is butt up

Silent sorrow
Tastes like tamarind

      Bare branches define the bank

      What if? Games
      Plague my mind

      What will it be like to die?

      The log is empty

I imagine those final moments –
cannot seem to resist playing out scenarios
Turning over the possibilities in my mind

      The bleeding heart bush barely blooms

Reactions

I randomly tell people.

Some brush it off. Skin cancer? What's the big deal?
Some recoil, not wanting to get close to the edge
of my mortality.

>A friend tells me that she is so terrified of melanoma
>that every time she sees a suspicious spot,
>she calls her doctor and demands to be seen that day!

Some reassure me that I will be fine.
I am drawn to this message.
It resonates with the fortune teller.

>I am plenty irritated with her at the moment.
>The small dark spot was there when she said "No cancer."

I think about the card: Wheel of Fortune
Risk, big payoffs, huge losses.

>Do I need to buy a vowel to have a long life?

>>I see the Fortune Teller smiling,
>>swaying to the music
>>flashing her Empress Tattoo.
>>"Long life", she says. "Long life."

>I feel ridiculously fine.

Maybe I could just stop drawing that black circle on my leg?

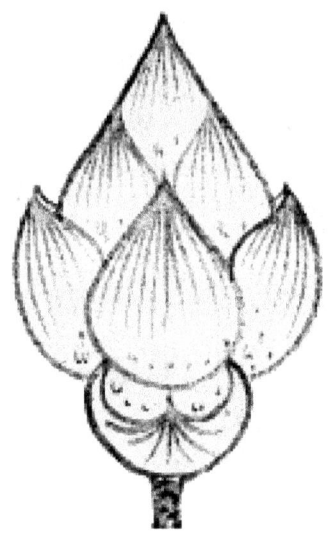

Tumor World

Red carpet madness
Offsets the sadness

    "Who are you wearing?"
        "Sharpie"
            How daring!
A model twirl
Signature whorl

Paparazzi pop and flash
Raising questions I don't ask

    "What's the stage?"

My smart phone searches, scan the web
for survival rates and tumor states

    There is Clark's level of invasion - *a new Disney ride?*
        Breslow's thickness or depth - *roller coaster romp, vertical drop*
            Mitotic rate - *a new kind of interest?*

    "What's the stage?"

The press persists
Asking questions I long to resist

    "WHAT'S THE STAGE?"

        Gathering evidence seems to suggest –

            "T1B" is my best guess.

One More Cup of Coffee

My surgery is scheduled: 11 AM
I shower: the night before and the morning of

> It's a germ thing
> Hibiclens
> 3 minutes on the skin

I check the paper work
look for the clause

> this is all a joke
> cosmic hoax

I'd really like a cup of coffee.

My daughter accompanies me to the hospital
She is 24: The designated responsible adult

> We both feign brave
> Will I be saved?

At the desk: There's a shift, low murmurs, and knowing looks.

I smell coffee – its aroma taunts me

The IV slips into my arm.

I have been betrayed by the fortune teller
Why didn't she tell me that I would need to act?

They wheel me through the doors into a cold white space

Winter

Firs unbent

Bittersweet
Orange heat

Deer dance
Brittle branch

Crunch

Snap

Howl

Tap

Blood stains
Silence wanes

Seasons turn
Sleigh bells yearn

- and yet ice forms

Post Op

I am in no pain
        Mountain top, bebop

My leg, though, aches for days
        Pain killers, classic thriller

There is a permanent dent in my calf
        Deep purge, slow dirge

I won't wear dresses again

Nick of Time

The results of the path report.
Cold seeps in.

I am no longer sure that I will have a long life.

My oncologist enters.
He seems serious.

    "The surgery was essential.
     There were more cells."
                        Breathe: long (in)
    "The borders are clear."
                        Breathe: life (out)

       "We got it in the nick of time."
       Bonnie Raitt's song swells in my head

    "This saved your life."

Staring at him, I babble.

    "I thought this whole thing ... was ridiculous ... overkill."

I look down and struggle
to connect the scar on my leg
with my mortality.

        Bonnie's voice fades

I jokingly tell him that I am considering a tattoo-
maybe the Wheel of Fortune card.

The doctor does not think this is funny.

Pathology – with a Nod to Coldplay's "Death and All His Friends"

Words wash over me
        Gentle tides lap the shore

Words hang in the air

More cells
        Float like clouds

Borders clear
                Horizons rise – disappear
                Buoy bells bob and cheer
                Amidst the fog
                Seaweed clogs
                Wraps and chokes
                Death's designer ocean cloak

Vigilance – an angry cure

Breathe deep
Release
Always on the precipice

Wondering what lurks beneath the stinking kelp.

Post Script: The Aftermath

Fine print reveals
Words not healed
Worst – best possible mess

Ulcerated, spreading
A slight shift
Might have brought a different rift

 Are you checking your lymph nodes?
 Yes - no ... am I supposed to?

Was I told this before?

Does it matter?

        Matter burns
        Fire swells
        Water quenches
        Wishing hell

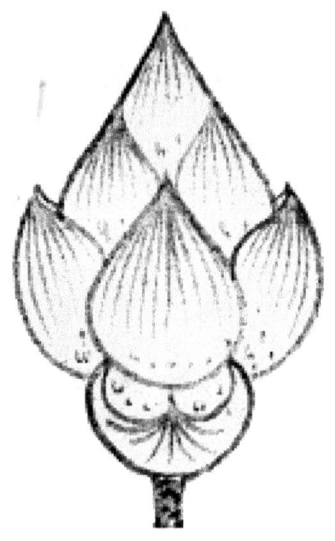

Peace in Ordinary Time

In between

A space
To breathe
No place
To leave

Lawn mowers drone
Willow moans

Soak in the heat
Sounds of the street
Wind whispers

Ripples

Tickles

Cool relief

Suspend disbelief

Senses stall
Mirrors, walls -
Deflect the sound

I am earth bound

Permissions

From the Penguin publication, I Heard God Laughing, copyright 1996 & 2006 by Daniel Ladinsky and used with his permission.

www.ingramcontent.com/pod-product-compliance
Lightning Source LLC
Chambersburg PA
CBHW061309040426
42444CB00010B/2571